Healthy Living

Protein Foods

by Vanessa Black

Bullfrog
Books

Ideas for Parents and Teachers

Bullfrog Books let children practice reading informational text at the earliest reading levels. Repetition, familiar words, and photo labels support early readers.

Before Reading

- Discuss the cover photo. What does it tell them?
- Look at the picture glossary together. Read and discuss the words.

Read the Book

- "Walk" through the book and look at the photos. Let the child ask questions. Point out the photo labels.
- Read the book to the child, or have him or her read independently.

After Reading

- Prompt the child to think more. Ask: How many servings of protein foods do you think you eat a day? What is your favorite protein food?

Bullfrog Books are published by Jump!
5357 Penn Avenue South
Minneapolis, MN 55419
www.jumplibrary.com

Copyright © 2017 Jump! International copyright reserved in all countries. No part of this book may be reproduced in any form without written permission from the publisher.

Library of Congress Cataloging-in-Publication Data

Names: Black, Vanessa, author.
Title: Protein foods / by Vanessa Black.
Description: Minneapolis, MN: Jump!, Inc. [2016]
Series: Healthy living
"Bullfrog Books are published by Jump!"
Audience: Ages 5–8. | Audience: K to grade 3.
Includes bibliographical references and index.
Identifiers: LCCN 2016028284 (print)
LCCN 2016029214 (ebook)
ISBN 9781620315460 (hardcover: alk. paper)
ISBN 9781620315811 (pbk.)
ISBN 9781624964947 (ebook)
Subjects: LCSH: Proteins in human nutrition
Juvenile literature. | Food of animal origin
Juvenile literature. | Nutrition—Juvenile literature.
Health—Juvenile literature.
Classification: LCC TX553.P7 B53 2016 (print)
LCC TX553.P7 (ebook) | DDC 641.3/08—dc23
LC record available at https://lccn.loc.gov/2016028284

Editor: Jenny Fretland VanVoorst
Book Designer: Molly Ballanger
Photo Researcher: Molly Ballanger

Photo Credits: All photos by Shutterstock except: iStock, 12; Thinkstock, 4.

Printed in the United States of America at Corporate Graphics in North Mankato, Minnesota.

Table of Contents

Power Foods

Sam has a big day.

He has a test.

How should he feed his brain?

Protein foods.

Protein helps you think.
It helps you work.

It helps you play.

What has protein?

Meat. Beans. Nuts. Fish. Eggs.

beans

meat

fish

nuts

egg

peanuts

Protein foods
are a good snack.

Yu has peanuts.

Kip has a beef stick.

Ivy has an egg.

13

Lunch?

Eat some protein.

Jo has salmon.

salmon

Sid has turkey.
Ana has beans.

Protein is good at dinner.
JT has tofu.

Samar has a burger.

Protein helps you grow.

It makes you strong.

Eat up!

Your Daily Protein

You need four servings of protein a day.

beef
Beef is the third most popular meat in the world, after pork (pig) and poultry (chicken, turkey, etc.).

salmon
Salmon is a popular protein food; much of the salmon people eat comes from fish farms.

lentils
Lentils come from a bushy plant, with two seeds to a pod; they come in a variety of colors.

eggs
Most of the eggs we eat are laid by chickens, but people eat turkey, duck, quail, and pheasant eggs as well.

Picture Glossary

beef
Meat from a steer, cow, or bull.

salmon
A large fish with pinkish-orange flesh.

protein
Chemicals found in animal-based foods, nuts, and beans that help the body grow.

tofu
A soft food made from soybeans.

Index

To Learn More

Learning more is as easy as 1, 2, 3.

1) Go to www.factsurfer.com

2) Enter "proteinfoods" into the search box.

3) Click the "Surf" button to see a list of websites.

With factsurfer.com, finding more information is just a click away.